Glitter and Grit

Jess Galatola

BookLeaf Publishing

India | USA | UK

Presentation by *BookLeaf Publishing*

Web: www.bookleafpub.com

E-mail: info@bookleafpub.com

ISBN: 9789358318210

First edition 2023

DEDICATION

To the beautiful, shiny beings in my universe, who make me a better human every day, thank you for sharing this planet with me.

ACKNOWLEDGEMENT

This collection of words is dedicated to my
mother.
She is the women who brought me into the
world and thanks to her love, praise, wisdom
and support, I have been able to face every
lesson life has to offer, with confidence, courage
and tenacity.
Love you, Mum.

PREFACE

"A life without glitter is no life at all." - Toni Collette

When I Came In

When I came in there was mother and blood.
Protection and life.
A love like no other,
concrete. Steadfast.

When I came in there was father and place.
Outside of mother's wisdom,
more set in the past.
Loving but separate.
Afraid of her wisdom but not of the task -
of moving us forward, with home and
possessions.
Money and purpose.
Stern. Little love lost.

When I came in there was brother and sister.
Older and busy.
Curious but bored.
Moments of doting battled adolescent
indulgence.
Baby cuddles were
less of a comfort and more of a chore.

When I came in there was music, synthetic
and outfits electric, with shoulder pad sleek.

Men looked like women and women like men,
bolder, androgynous, unlike eras before.
Sex was invented in new ways, I'm sure.

When I came in the times were a changing,
the roller skates moving from fashion to trend.
Next, blades and a Walkman
socks that were slouchy, denim that was
doubled.
And hair stood on end.

When I came in, my soul was an old one,
a live wire of memories,
of lives from before.
In the haze of the other place,
not quite yet in this world.
Figuring it all out before knowing for sure.

When I came in, I had purpose and reason,
body, mind and meaning.
Innocence peeking through chubby human skin.
And I looked at my mother
regarded my father
met brother and sister
and took it all in.

A Swing in the Sun

Memories of a simple childhood, spent well,
come down to this:

A rusty swing in a loved backyard,
beneath a tree so large
it housed a cubby, all the way round.
An eco-house for gangs of kids
to climb and hideout amongst the planks and
leaves.
I cut my hair in that cubby house
and hid the evidence in a hole in the tree.

Legs hanging over the swing, too chubby and
short to touch the ground.
Cotton dress in an 80s cut and hair the shape of a
bowl.
A mouth rejoicing at the wonder of apricot jam
on white bread.
White bread? A mother would be in jail for
white bread sandwiches today!
The flood of sunshine on my face causing
intricate lace shadows, tattooed on my skin,
tracing lace across my face, arms and bare legs,
whilst I swung on that old, rusty swing.

Giggling, always giggling
At another child - a cousin, a cat, or a bird.
A grandparent with false teeth.
Or at absolutely nothing at all.
Imagine that!

Nothing to entertain
but a swing and some sun,
and the wonder of a tree
and the taste of mother nature's nectar on my
tongue.

Simple memories from a simpler time, when I
was young.

Fat

5

Don't eat that!
You've had enough.
Good god, girl, must you always think of food?
No more.
It's not good for you.
You'll get FAT.
And you wouldn't want that!

Cabbage Patch Baby

When I was four, I owned a Cabbage Patch doll,
her name was Augustus,
she was my sweetheart.

And I mothered her wisely,
clothed bathed and dressed her,
and pushed her around in her little doll cart.

Until one day my brother
swooped in and attacked her,
pulling and ripping her doll arms apart.

I cried, Weeping Willow,
until my mother patched her arms,
tenderly she mended my doll a fresh start.

But I never forgot
the actions of her aggressor,
at the tender age of four I evoked the black arts.

I planted food in his bedroom,
crude but effective, it molded-
and smoldered, and smelled of off farts.

For though he was older

and stronger, not brighter,
one thing he forgot was at four – I was smart.

And while he bitterly complained
of the smell in his bedroom, Augustus
smiled sweetly, acknowledging my part.

And for the rest of that year,
I carried on loving my
sweet cabbage baby, with all of my heart.

Fat Part Two

Little girls should be little
And big girls should try harder.

Boom bada boom.
Boom bada boom
taunts the older brother.

Don't you want to be like the others?
Don't you want to fit into your clothes?
Don't you want to be normal?
No! You don't want to eat those!

Boom bada boom.
Boom bada boom,
I'm a walking earthquake.

Hey fatty, can you catch me?
God, you're so fat.
Why don't you go and eat your feelings?
No! You can't eat that!

Boom bada boom.
Boom bada boom -
the anxious sound
of my embarrassed heart.

Don't pick her! She can't run fast.
Don't pick her, she's too chubby.
Don't pick her she's not worthy.
She's not pretty… but God she's funny.

Boom bada boom.
Boom bada boom.
The explosion of unworthiness inside me.

Service Station Flowers

Nothing says romance
like a wilted bunch of service station flowers,
drooping with the promise of a terrible evening.
Hastily stowed beneath the glove box
of her first boyfriend's car.
He shoved them at her, now.
Into the hands of a girl expecting Hallmark
on her first Valentines date.
An unapologetic explanation
"I nearly forgot"
punctuated the posy
better than any service station card ever could.
The girl took the flowers,
strangled in plastic and crushed like her hopes.
A cloud of decay shrouded the shrubs
and three persistent midges,
floated gracefully around the lifeless buds
humming with the promise of a rotten evening.
A clumsy, last minute slapped together evening.
The girl lay the blooms on her lap and
a pungent rim of water
from the fetid stems
seeped a damp stain into her pretty dress,
and soaked her heart with dread.
Nothing says romance

like a wilted bunch of service station flowers,
a putrid symbol of things to come
and an omen to run.

Cheap Date

The plastic covering of her flowers
perfectly coordinated with the plastic tablecloth
the girl ate off that night,
at dinner.
A cheap date
at a local fish and chip shop,
owned by a Korean Queen
who cared more for music than she did for fish
and chips.
 The Queen took to the stage, in front of the
crumbed cod,
every fifteen minutes
to belt out Madonna and Celine.
In broken English
and discordant harmony.
The girl pushed her fish to the side of her dish
and wished with all of her Valentine heart
that she had gone out to dinner with her
girlfriends.

Cloaked

She wraps a cloak around her to hide away the
truth.
She fills her pockets with heavy burdens that
weigh her down.

She pulls the chord, tight, around her throat,
to block the words from spilling out.
She hides beneath the folds of fabric
and gives over her power to the weight of the
world,
that presses down upon the cloak.

The negative space between the cloak and the
outside world,
infiltrating, intertwining and intoxicating
the space within the cloak
with more negative space
until every space is negative
and the girl. Can't. Breathe.

Once comforting protection,
now stifling and suffocating.
It snares and traps her.
Why not take the cloak off? She thinks.

As the weight pushes her down into the wet,
dense earth
where the worms wiggle and oxygenate the soil.

She smiles at the worms.

I Didn't Mean to Scrape Your Car

I didn't mean to scrape your car.
I was leaving for work, hungover.
I'm sorry.
I was so tired and
my mind was somewhere else.
I really should have let you drive me to work
but I was upset.

You had parked me in. So close.
I didn't want to wake you.
I'm sorry.
I didn't mean to scrape your car.

Did you mean to scrape my heart?
When you told me you were seeing other people.
Just like that.
You reversed over my heart
and scraped the inside of my lungs
and left me with no air.

I'm sorry.
I didn't mean to scrape your car.
It really was an accident.

Disney Princes

Little girls are sold Disney princes.
Brave and bold and rich.
Romance is delivered through soft kisses,
valiant acts and generous gifts.

Truth be told,
the kisses are unsolicited,
received without consent.
Valiant acts –
roughly yanking a young woman's hair
because –
she likes it like that.
And generous gifts are only granted
if the shoe fits.

Little girls are sold Disney princes.
Perfect hair and chiselled chins.
Muscled, tanned and toned,
and guess what? The prince always wins.

Truth be told,
the perfect hair
starts falling out at 38.
The chiselled chin nothing more
than the preferred angle

of princes on dating apps.
Muscles, tanned and toned?
Well, that's a lie. But who really cares?
Because no matter what, the prince always wins.

Little girls are sold Disney princes,
but they are not taught how to return them.
Sold a dream, not a reality,
princes are just two dimensional men.

Truth be told,
The Prince might not be into you
if you are not a Disney Princess.
Or worse.
The Prince might be jealous if you are a
Princess.
Intimidated by your brain
and threatened by your charm.
Or worse.
If the Prince deems that you are not a princess
he might in fact,
deem you a villain.
One to be fought and tamed and conquered.

Little girls are not told,
that there is more to the princess dream,
that they might prefer to be a villain –
or a beautiful and powerful queen.

Truth be told,
Disney villains are always women
with strong opinions,
and powerful minds
and magical abilities
who make princes feel
small and
weak.
Or worse,
inadequate and
ashamed.
Or worse.
Angry.

Little girls should be told
they don't need a prince
and they needn't be a princess or a villain
because, who are they trying to convince?

Truth be told,
I am a woman,
not a little girl.
I'd rather be left alone and misunderstood,
than chosen by a prince.
In fact, by choice
I am happily in my
Disney villain phase.

Always Running

Always running.
Or always waiting.
Never in between.

Either desperately pushing my way through
to seize the moment and claim my seat by the
window,
knowing that the series of events that follow
will be relaxed,
orderly, punctual.

Or, waiting hopelessly, desperately
watching the tracks
feeling the energy that just passed by,
only moments ago.

Thinking about all of the moments in life that
will be suspended
or pushed backwards.
A sliding doors moment.

Running.
Heart beating, steps pounding,
which side of the train door will I be on today?

Ah. Of course.
Just missed it.
Waiting.

Seether

Seething is a burning bile,
poisoning your blood stream.
Sulfuric acid through your pours.
An active volcano
threatening to spew out pus
and noxious fumes.
Lava and angry ash in your throat,
ears, nostrils.

Seething is the cold, nitric gas that filters in.
A layer of icy sleet that sets and cracks into
place
around a hardened, gnarled, heart.
Arteries plugged with rot and scraped with
shards of broken glass.
Stalagmites growing like capillaries,
fragmented, severe and grotesque.
The liquid of loathing,
hot white fury
or cold black bitterness
noxious gas –
is chemical warfare of the body.

Seething is sickness. It's cancer.
It's an eternity of anxious loops

that sink into every vacant space and
it's the aggressive release of fury into the void.
A pit of anguish and descending despair.
A sinkhole.
It's the death of one feeling and the birth of
another.
The end of something and the start of another
thing.

But no seether escapes, unscathed.

Maybe Just Don't Leave the House

Maybe the reason we are afraid to leave the
house
to go for a walk, and clear our minds, is -
the shadow of a man lurking in our minds,
threatening to close in on us.

His heavy footsteps on the pavement,
footsteps that seem to echo to the beat of our
own heart
as they approach.
Louder.
Closer.

Or the car that circles the street
again and again
until it slows down. Stops.
His face, leers out of the window.
Or worse.

His words -
threatening.
Uninvited.
Predatory words.

Maybe it's the fear of assault,
insults,
misogyny,
rape,
murder?

Maybe it's the thought, alone,
that's stops us in our tracks.

Maybe that's why we just don't leave the house.

I am not afraid to leave the house at night, for
fear of a woman.
Only men.
Hashtag not all men?

Well.
Which ones then?
How could any woman know for sure?
Just as I feared.

Maybe just don't leave the house.

You Are Frost

Lately I'm lamenting,
How quickly time does pass.
I wish it away and then wish it back
As it passes by, too fast.

I love the feel of a little hand, folded neatly into
mine.
And the squeals and shrieks of a little guy, who
loves his tickle time.

The funny little things they say, when the
muddle up their words,
The way they race across the field, chasing after
birds.

Their curious smile on their bashful face, as they
realize something new.
I know their favourite colours, when they
change from red to blue.

I love to watch their sleepy faces, tilt towards
my own.
I love to watch them play together in our family
home.

Even when it's really tough and all our tempers
rise.
Even when words can't be taken back, even
when we cry.

I wouldn't trade a single one of these moments
now-
when I think of you, every now and then, I
always wonder. How?

How could you turn your back? Not on me, but
on every childhood moment?
How you don't regret the time you've lost, how
your heart continues to lay dormant.

Do you feel sad because you don't have a tiny
hand to hold?
Do you regret the fact that you'll be alone, when
you eventually grow old?

Do you know their favourite colours or about
their deepest fears?
Have you ever felt your own heart ache, when
you wipe away their tears?

Don't you wish you could have been there, to
kiss them every day?

To smile at their laughter and the silly things
they say.

To know them, in and out, through and through,
as if you share their heart?
Instead, you just erased them in search of your
new start.

I often wonder if you're own heart, is made of
iron or stone.
Because your frosty choices are like a burn I've
never known.

I really can't believe that you just gave your
children up.
That you dragged their hearts down with you,
without giving any fucks.

And I really have to wonder, one day, will you
feel regret?
For the childhoods that you missed and the love
you'll never get.

Sadly. I truly doubt it.
For you are frost.
You are cold
Stone cold.
Jack Frost.
You don't know what you've lost.

But I do.

She Has Walked With Me

She has walked with me
across the Summer grass-
late and apathetic
on our way to class.

She has walked with me,
through adolescent stages -
setting awkward, girly history
on early pages.

She has walked with me,
a warrior with each step.
Through black and white swooping wings
metallic beak and relentless pecks.

She has walked with me
through the phase of silly, hopeful girls.
Before we knew what we now know,
before our futures unfurled.

She has walked with me
through my doubts and fears, all the times I've
felt unsure.
Never, ever judging,
always soothing, calm, assured.

She has walked with me
through pregnancies: exhausted, fat and tired.
We laughed together, in those days,
at all we had acquired.

She has walked with me,
holding babies, sharing nappies and broken
conversations.
During times that moved in slow motion, or
stood completely still,
or sped right past our expectations.

She has walked with me
through heavier times, when I was lost and
slipped away.
She could see me disappearing.
So, she held my hand and stayed.

She has walked with me
through heartache, and it may have hurt her
more.
To watch me reach into the darkness,
To pick my heart up off the floor.

She has walked with me through rebirth -
When I found myself again.
Perhaps she met me anew, again,
the girl who had always been her friend.

She has walked with me in past lives,
other galaxies and through black holes.
Because there is not a single doubt
that I truly know her soul.

She will walk with me forever,
every day, week, year, that we have left.
And I hope she knows that she's the reason,
that I feel truly blessed!

I Forgive You

I forgive you,
because I know longer wish to carry the burden
of a twisted face,
a knotted stomach,
a brittle heart
or an anxious mind.

I forgive you because there were two of us in the
marriage.
I forgive you because holding on to blame serves
no purpose.
I forgive you because I have managed to find
happiness,
in spite of great sorrow.

I forgive you because you gave me the gift of
opening my heart and home,
to real love, joy, strength, courage, family and
magic.
These gifts were not from you. These things
came after.
Because you took your lack lustre cloud away,
hanging heavily over your shoulders, now,
where I fear it shall remain until the end of your
days.

I forgive you because I have gained so much
more than I lost.
I forgive you because my brain impatiently waits
for order,
my heart demands transformation
and my soul wishes to fly faster, higher and
more freely on its way
back to me.

I forgive you because I want my boys to learn
that I am strong and compassionate.
I forgive you because you are human.
I forgive you because I no longer love you.
I forgive you because forgiveness is the truest
way to heal myself.

Only one thing remains that I will not forgive.
Because that one thing… is unforgivable,
and because that thing is not mine to forgive.
The rest - is history.
Dust in the wind.
It's gone.
I release it.
The universe takes it.
And I dance forward,
again.

Found Again

When the light shines bright, through the cracks
everything that once felt lost,
is found again.

At first you blink,
the light hurts your eyes,
you don't want to see it.

But you get used to it – the light.

It warms your face and tickles your skin
and reminds you that its time to get up,
and find yourself again.

Full Potential

I am a mother, strong and proud.
I am a feminist, fierce and loud.
I have a career and I help others
I have friends and we support each other.
I've been married, I've been divorced.
I've learned to choose me, even when it feels
forced.
I know who I am and I trust where I'm going.
I believe in learning and I believe in knowing.
I am kind, supportive, unique and true.
I say what I think and I mean what I do.
I am successful, a published author.
I'm an accomplished woman and a proud mum's
daughter .
She loves me so much, my adoring mother
no doubtedly more than any other.
She builds me up and says she's proud
So why do these words, ring so loud?
Once you lose the weight,
you will reach your full potential!
That, dear Mother, is inconsequential.
The words reach for shame,
and provoke deep conditioning.
Of Patriarchal ideals
that require repositioning.

And blame -
blame, the weight gain
for it holds you back …
can't achieve your full potential
till you're no longer fat.
Wow.
Imagine that!
But you know what?
That's total crap.

Glitter's in Our Blood

Are you a mermaid?
Whispered the little girl with the confetti
freckles,
sprinkled across her nose.

I am part mermaid, I confessed.
Her eyes sparkled like sea glass.
Cool.

How did you guess I'm a mermaid?
She tilted her head and crinkled the confetti on
her nose.
It's because you have glitter eyes,
your makeup is really pretty.

Oh?
I say.
Yes.
She says,
pleased that she has pinpointed
the feature that best affirms my mermaid
geneology,

You are very wise, I tell her.
She nods and without missing a beat and says.

That's because I'm a mermaid too.

Ah.
I smile.
Cool.

Well. Takes one to know one, I conclude.
How did you know, she asks.
Because of your confetti freckles.
The confetti crinkles again, nearly sliding off her
face.
It's magical, I tell her.
She whispers one more time, before she moves
to the carpet to play with the tea set.
Glitter is in our blood.
And this time I am the one who smiles,
Glitter eyes crinkling at the corners.
The young ones are so wise.

My Little Boys

Slugs and snails and puppy dog tails,
they say.
That's what boys are made of.
But little boys are made of sunshine,
damp earth, sweetness
and adventure.

Boys will be boys,
they say.
But little boys are little people
and little people are all very different.
Not a single one the same.
Children have their own, magical way of being.

Boys are boisterous
you can't hold them back,
they say.
Little boys can be boisterous,
but so can little girls.
Why do we point out the difference?

Little boys curl their fingers around your hair
while they cry into your shoulder,
silver trails on your sleeve, their
heartaches mumbled into your ear.

Little boys smile shyly, warmly
and ever so sweetly.
They hold up their artworks
proudly.
Artworks made just for you.

Little boys tell you freely that they love you,
and they mean it in buckets and spades.
They might curse you out,
fiercely rage, out of control
but when told that feelings are okay-
they find their way back to the feeling of love.

For little boys are the future.
My little boys
are the future.

Witch

Witch?
Oh to be so lucky.
For a witch is a powerful woman
who snaps photos of clouds
and sighs at the moon
and breaths in the salt of the ocean
and breaths out powerful manifestations.

She wears her hair wild
and her pockets deep.
Deep enough to carry smooth, worry stones
and glitter for the fairies
and a lucky button
and a piece of paper with a single name etched
in ink
and sealed with dirt
from the crossroads, where two dogs quarreled.

For words are spells and names are promises,
prophesies and paraphernalia
best saved for a rainy day.
Witch!

A magical goddess
who lives by the beat of her own heartbeat

off her own, beaten track,
tuned into the frequency of the universe,
set to the spirit station.
Witch.
A woman.
Unafraid of her own power,
who knows who she is,
believes in her own magic
and is wise
enough to do life her way.